SMART BRAIN RIGHT BRAIN

An Introduction to the Internet

Om KIDZ
An imprint of Om Books International

Om Kidz | Om Books International

Reprinted in 2023

Corporate & Editorial Office
A-12, Sector 64, Noida 201 301
Uttar Pradesh, India
Phone: +91 120 477 4100
Email: editorial@ombooks.com
Website: www.ombooksinternational.com

Sales Office
107, Ansari Road, Darya Ganj
New Delhi 110 002, India
Phone: +91 11 4000 9000
Email: sales@ombooks.com

Author: Shweta Sinha
Editor: Kirti Pathak
Art & Design: Anshuman Pandey, Gaurav Bhandari, Harish Arya

ISBN: 978-93-52768-38-7

Printed in India

10 9 8 7 6 5 4 3 2

CONTENTS

1. What Is the Internet?

Is it a magical world? Is it what makes the computer work? Is it something that comes from space and is full of cool videos, games and movies? Or is it some big computer hidden in a well-guarded secret cave?

What is this internet?

Where is it?

What is it made of?

Let's pretend you could link together the computers in your school. This will create a computer network. All computers have some information saved on them. From one computer, you can now see the information shared on the others.

The internet is something like that. Only, the internet is a network of millions of computers worldwide! It lets us send information from one computer to another anywhere in the world.

DID YOU KNOW? 'Internet' comes from the word 'inter-networking'.

Where is the Internet?

The Internet is everywhere in the world, except for some places like the South Pole. It is a vast network of computers and other devices connected to each other. The internet is all the hardware that make up this vast network.

DID YOU KNOW? There is a 3G cell service and internet capabilities even on the top of Mount Everest!

The Internet is a virtual world that exists on computers. It is not the real world that you see around you. Your real world consists of your school and your neighbourhood. It consists of people like your teachers, friends and family. The internet is a tool people use to get information.

POCKET FACT

Computers on the internet connect using phone lines, satellites, radio links and by many other ways.

Internet Services

How do people use the internet?

- Email - This is one of the most popular services on the internet. You can use email to stay in touch with your friends and family.

- File transfer - Internet is most useful if you want to share large-sized files with others.

- Online chat and phone calls - Internet lets you talk to your friends far away.

- World Wide Web - This is where you watch videos, play games, and do research for your school projects.

DID YOU KNOW?

Today, there are more users on the internet than there are people who watch TV.

2. What Constitutes the Internet?

Clients

Clients are all the devices on the internet used to access internet services. We use clients to view pictures and videos, download files and to send emails. Laptops, desktops, phones, tablets and even some TVs are clients.

POCKET FACT

We spend more time browsing on mobile devices than on computers.

Server

Servers provide the internet services we use, like emails and the world wide web. A server is essentially a powerful computer. It is directly connected to the internet.

DID YOU KNOW? Servers that host web pages for the world wide web are called 'Web Servers'.

Router

Routers are devices that 'route' data on the internet. When you send a letter by mail, the letter hops from post office to post office, until it is delivered at its address. In the same way, 'routers' guide information to their destination.

Every device on the internet has a computer number. Routers use this number to locate the device on the internet. The computer number is called its Internet Protocol (IP) Address. It is written as four numbers separated by dots - 192.168.0.1

POCKET FACT

Computers on the internet talk to each other using a language called TCP/IP (Transmission Control Protocol/Internet Protocol).

3. The History of Internet

Believe it or not, the internet was created as a result of two nations trying to outdo each other.

1957

The Soviet Union (now Russia) launched Sputnik, the first manmade rocket in space. This scared the USA. They did not want to lose the race of technology.

1962

The USA was also scared that the Soviet Union would attack them and destroy their telephone system. Researchers working for the US Government Defence Department came up with the idea of a computer network that could share information.

1968

The first message was delivered between two computers. The network was called ARPANet then.

1971

Email was invented.

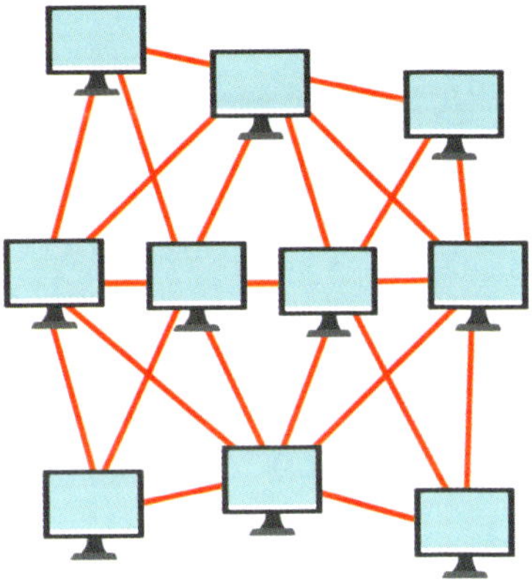

1974

The first time the term 'Internet' was used for this computer network. Big businesses, universities and other researchers joined this network. They made a web of networks.

1991

The world wide web was finally made available to the public.

DID YOU KNOW?

In the beginning, computers made direct calls to each other to connect, just like making a telephone call.

4. The World Wide Web

What is your favourite activity on the internet?

Is it watching videos and movies?

Listening to songs again and again?

Or playing your favourite game?

When you're doing any of these, you are actually using the World Wide Web. We access the World Wide Web using a software called a 'browser', like the Internet Explorer (IE), Google Chrome and Mozilla Firefox.

POCKET FACT

Safari, Chrome and Firefox Focus are some of the web browsers for mobile phones.

Often people refer to the World Wide Web as the 'Internet', but the two are not the same thing. Internet is the way computers connect with each other. It is the hardware.

The World Wide Web ("WWW" or "The Web") is only a part of the internet. It is one of the many services available on the internet.

DID YOU KNOW?

YouTube and Google are two of the millions of websites on the web.

What is the web made of?

The web is a collection of Web Pages. Your web browser uses the internet to show you web pages. A web page is simply a document written in a special computer language, called HTML. A web browser can read and understand this language. A website is a collection of one or more web pages linked together.

DID YOU KNOW? The world's first website is still online. You can check it out at info.cern.ch!

Imagine the web as a city of skyscrapers. Each building in the city is a web server that stores web pages. If you want your own website, all you do is rent a room in one of the buildings. Then move in your web pages and organise them in an orderly fashion. This is just like setting up your furniture in the room.

Your room has an address. Others can use this address to visit your website. This address is called - URL (Uniform Resource Locator). It is an easy way to remember the address for a webpage, like http:// www.google.com. Can you guess what the 'www' in the address stands for? It stands for 'World Wide Web'.

POCKET FACT

There can be an unlimited number of URLs as there is no limitation to a name.

History of the World Wide Web

In 1989, Sir Tim Berners-Lee invented the WWW at CERN in Geneva, Switzerland. He was a scientist and wanted to find an easy way for scientists to share information. Internet was already available. So he wrote a computer language, HTML, to link internet pages to other pages. He created the first ever website, the first ever web server and also the first ever web browser.

- The web became available to the public in 1991.
- In 1992, the first web server outside Europe was set up in the USA.
- By 1993, people began using the WWW. They started creating their own websites.
- In 1994, access to the internet reached homes through telecom companies.

DID YOU KNOW? Sir Timothy John Berners-Lee is also known as TimBL.

Sir Tim Berners-Lee gave away the World Wide Web for free. This allowed everyone to use the web and not just the scientists. It helped people connect with each other and get information quickly.

Today, people use the web to share their work and thoughts through blogs, social media and videos. The WWW is used for everything - from ordering food, checking the weather and sharing news to even starting revolutions!

POCKET FACT

World Wide Web Consortium (W3C) is an organisation founded by Sir Lee that makes sure the web continues to work and develop.

5. Activity: Make Your Own Webpage

You too can build your own web page using HTML
(Hyper Text Markup Language). In HTML, you simply add tags to your text.

Try this simple web page:

```
<html>

<head>

<title>My first web page</title>

</head>

<body>

<h1> This is my web page </h1>

<p> I am learning to build my own web pages.

<b>YAY!</b> </p>

</body>

</html>
```

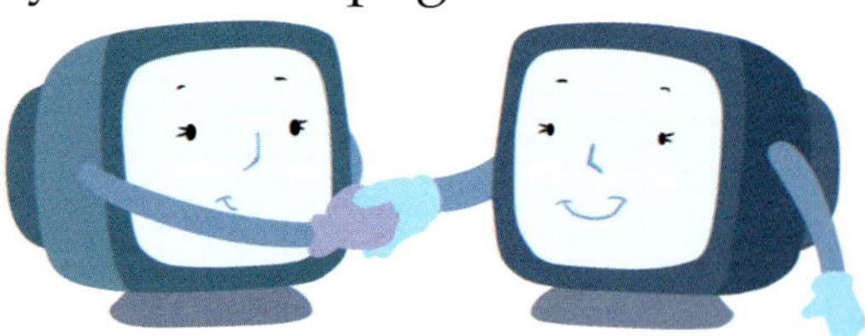

1. Open 'notepad' on your computer.
2. Type the above code.
3. Save the file on your computer as 'mypage.html'. You can choose any other name too. But make sure you put 'html' after the dot.

4. Now open this file in a web browser.

This is what you will see:

POCKET FACT

https://www.w3schools.com/ is a good online resource to learn to code in HTML.

6. Different Ways to Communicate Online

- **Email:** This is like sending a digital letter. All you need is an email address. These text based messages travel almost instantly. You can even attach pictures, documents and other files in your email. Emails are useful when you want to share your project work or homework with your teachers and friends.

- **Instant Messaging:** You can use a variety of apps to send text messages to other people. This is useful when you want to send quick messages to your friends and family.

- **Video Calling:** You may have used a computer to talk to your friends and family. Unlike a phone call, you can see the other person on a video call. To make a video call, you need a webcam on your computer.

- **Blog**: A blog is a website that people use to share their thoughts. You can think of a blog as an online journal. You can write stuff for other people to read. You can even post videos and photos on a blog.

- **Newsletter:** A newsletter is like a digital newspaper that arrives by email, instead of on your doorstep.

- **Social Media:** These are websites that allow people to connect with others and share photos and other content. Facebook, Twitter and Instagram are social media platforms. People use social media to create social networks.

7. Staying Safe Online

What are the risks?

- **Privacy -** Your online information can be seen by anyone - even strangers.
- **Permanency -** Once you put something on the internet, it stays there for a long time, even after you delete them.
- **Trolling -** Some people use social media to hurt or bully other people.
- **Catfishing -** People can steal your information and pretend to be you by creating a fake profile. Other people may think it's your profile even though it is not.
- **Virus -** Attachments in emails can have harmful software that steal data or damage your computer. This is true for the stuff you download from websites too.

Golden rules to staying safe:

- Do not share your address, phone number, school details or password on the internet.
- Only accept 'friend requests' from people you know in real life.
- Ask an adult before sharing photos or other media.
- Be polite about what you write. Do not use rude words.
- Block anyone you don't feel comfortable connecting with.

- Never agree to meet someone you only know online.
- Do not download stuff from emails or website unless you are sure of it. Consult an adult before doing so.
- Finally, do not spend too much time online. Go outside and play with your real friends. That is even more fun.

8. The Future of Internet

The internet hasn't been around very long. Yet, we cannot live without it today. It has changed a lot since it was invented.

Cloud Computing

Until now, we used the hardware and software sitting inside our computers. As we needed more and more, the box became too small. So now, we use computer services provided over the internet.

Cloud computing is like using electricity. We plug into the internet to receive services, like storage or computing power. Like with electricity, we pay for what we use.

POCKET FACT

Sir Tim Berners-Lee believes there are unlimited ways to using the internet. All you need is a little imagination.

Internet of Things

This is perhaps the most exciting idea of internet usage. Can you imagine your car talking to your house? Or your refrigerator suggesting you recipes? Well, these are examples of an idea called the 'Internet of Things (IoT)'.

In future, dumb objects like cars, refrigerators, washing machines and air conditioners will have internet access. Your car can then tell your house to turn the lights on, even while you are on your way home. The IoT is a smart technology that can make our lives simpler.

POCKET FACT

Researchers believe by 2020 there will be over 26 billion devices connected to the internet.

Let's Get Active

Unscramble the words to get the correct answer:

1. __________ is a vast network of computers.

ERINTNTE

2. __________ guide information between devices on the internet.

STOURRE

3. Sending an email is like sending a ________ letter.

TGADLII

4. Firefox, Opera, Chrome, and Safari are types of __________

WSSORREB

5. A __________ is a newspaper that comes via email.

TTEELREWNS

Match the following:

1. Video Call — (a) 

2. Website URL — (b)

3. Sir Tim Berners-Lee — (c) 172.217.167.228

4. Sputnik (Russian man-made rocket) — (d) 

5. Facebook (Social Media) — (e) http://www.kiddle.co

6. IP Address — (f) 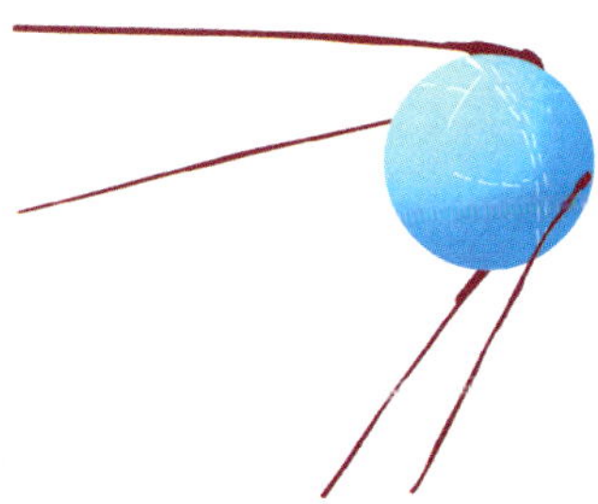

True or False

1. The World Wide Web is the same thing as the Internet. (True/False)

2. Servers provide the services we use on the internet. (True/False)

3. A mobile phone connected on the internet is called a client. (True/False)

4. Sir Tim Berners-Lee invented the internet. (True/False)

5. A website is a collection of web pages. (True/False)

6. In cloud computing, computers connect to the clouds in the sky. (True/False)

How Cyber smart are you?

1. Which of these emails will you open and which will you delete?

From	Subject	
Christina	How are you?	
abcd@zzyyxx.co	Hi! from Tommy	
prizes@lotto.ru	You have won $10,000!	

Hint: Only open emails from people you know.

2. You are checking out a cool new website. Tick the information you think is OK to give out online.

- First name
- Last name
- Nickname
- Phone number
- Email address
- Home address
- School name
- Credit card details

3. Your friends offer to share their username and password to a website you want to use. What will you do?

- Use their login information.
- Tell a parent and a teacher that your friend has been handing out passwords.

Hint: Never share passwords.

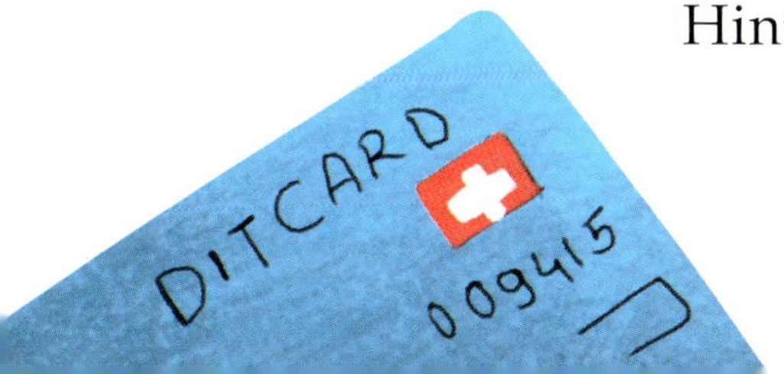

GLOSSARY

Blog	a website that is used like a diary or journal
Communicate	share or exchange information, news, or ideas
Computing power	how fast a machine can perform an operation
Digital	technology that is primarily used with new physical communications media
Hardware	part of a computer that you can see and touch
Invent	to create something new that no one has created before
Network	a group or system of interconnected people or things
Organisation	an organised group of people with a particular purpose, such as a business or government department
Permanency	how long something exists for
Social media	a website or service where people talk to, or network with other people
Software	a set of instructions and associated documentation that tells a computer what to do
Storage	a device for recording (storing) information (data)
Technology	the application of scientific knowledge for practical purposes
Virtual	not physically existing as such but made by software to appear to do so
Webcam	a video camera that connects to a computer

ANSWERS

Page 28. (1) Internet (2) Routers (3) Digital (4) Browsers (5) Newsletter

Page 29. 1. (d) 2. (e) 3. (a) 4. (f) 5. (b) 6. (c)

Page 30. (1) False; (2) True; (3) True; (4) False; (5) True; (6) False

Page 31. Do not give out - Last name, School name, Phone number, Credit card or Home address.